D1736676

DAVID MUENCH

Vast & Intimate
CONNECTING WITH THE NATURAL WORLD

TEXT BY LAWRENCE W. CHEEK

Arizona Highways
BOOKS

Book Designer: MARY WINKELMAN VELGOS

Photography Editor: RICHARD MAACK

Book Editor: BOB ALBANO

Copy Editor: PK PERKIN McMAHON

www.arizonahighways.com

Publisher: Win Holden / Managing Editor: Bob Albano / Associate Editor: PK Perkin McMahon / Associate Editor: Evelyn Howell
Art Director: Mary Winkelman Velgos / Director of Photography: Peter Ensenberger / Production Director: Cindy Mackey

Photographs ©2002 by David Muench
Essays ©2002 by Lawrence W. Cheek

DEDICATION
For Joyce Rockwood and Josef
Muench, my parents, who brought me
a world both vast and intimate.
— *David Muench*

Contents

PREVIOUS PAGE / A penlight focuses on the intimacy of a barrel cactus, and a setting sun casts a purple glow over Saguaro National Park near Tucson.

OPPOSITE PAGE / The impressionist school influences this image of Oak Creek near Sedona.

Vast & Intimate

INTRODUCTION: SEEING NATURE'S PATTERNS AND RELATIONSHIPS

*Moses Kaldor had always loved mountains; they made him feel nearer
to the God whose nonexistence he still sometimes resented.*
— *Arthur C. Clarke*
The Songs of Distant Earth

What do we learn when we look at a mountain? Or at a creek on that mountain, or at a mosaic of pebbles in that creek?

The obvious answers come easily: We learn light, color, form, texture, movement.

If we look more intently, or (perish the word) studiously, we learn about community. We observe an ecology in which all the elements nurture and threaten and devour each other and create a rabble of ongoing miracles out of the chaos. A storm over the mountain raises a creek; the creek relieves a sycamore's thirst; the sycamore shelters a Steller's jay; the sun breaks out and the jay flits away to become a hawk's dinner. As Emerson said, nature is no sentimentalist.

Still, this is only Biology 101, the mechanics of the food chain, a subject readily digested. What can we learn in nature beyond science?

In 1987, several thousand people flocked to the red rock country around Sedona, Arizona, for a metaphysical circus billed as the Harmonic Convergence. They meditated, prayed, chanted, and held hands in circles that were intended to draw up the mother energy of the Earth. A few reportedly bought tickets to sit on a rock that was shortly expected to zoom away to the galaxy of Andromeda. Many of the Convergers were earnestly seeking a

LAWRENCE W. CHEEK

ABOVE / David Muench explores beauty.
FOLLOWING PAGES / A thunderstorm over the Santa Rita Mountains splashes the landscape south of Tucson with color and water.

spiritual experience; some were certifiable cranks. But what it all illustrated, aside from the fact that earthly rocks do not casually launch themselves into space, is that landscape has extraordinary power over the human imagination and spirit.

"Begin with belief in a place that is still mostly earth and sky, a time-scented garden where nature is foremost and rocks are truth," wrote Robert Leonard Reid in *America, New Mexico*. The word *belief* is the centerpiece here, and it grows best in a vessel filled with observation and experience.

So if we learn to look *really* intently and intelligently and receptively, what do we discover? A fuller understanding of Nature, certainly, giving us a deeper richness and meaning. A spiritual connection with something greater than ourselves, possibly. In my own case, an examination of my conflicted relationship with Nature, a tangle of love and fear and increasing sorrow at how my voracious species is chewing it up.

My friend David Muench has cycled through all these experiences, and one thing more: He has discovered art in the meaning of Nature.

I choose that last verb pointedly. Most people with a camera *take* photographs; David *discovers* photographs. He exhibits an astounding gift for seeing patterns and relationships in the landscape that escape most of us.

After years of hiking canyons and mountains with him and standing around while he putters with his paleolithic Linhof 4x5 view camera, I've come to understand how he does it: He has a personal quality perhaps best called *receptivity*.

On a wilderness trail he exudes the wide-eyed wonder of a child tasting chocolate for the first time. Sometimes, as we hop boulders over a throwaway creek, he'll stop cold, transfixed by a mosaic of marble-sized cobblestones, the ripples in the water casting striations of shadows over them. He takes unrestrained joy in finding such patterns; they are Nature's art and they are everywhere for those with receptivity.

There are days with lousy light — a cloudless summer day, the sun virtually bleaching the sky — but in David's world there are no wastelands, no places so bleak they have nothing to show us.

Not many of us can learn photography at David's level, or write about Nature with the serrated wit of an Edward Abbey, but we can improve our receptivity — which may lead us to remarkable new insights. Three simple recommendations:

• Walk more patiently. Health clubs are for cardio workouts; mountains are for learning.

• Walk more thoughtfully. "You must walk like a camel," Thoreau punned wickedly, "which is said to be the only beast which ruminates while walking."

• Leave expectations home. If we plan on a pleasantly sunny day, and it rains instead, disappointment will smother the chance to receive the land on its own terms.

For this book, David has walked patiently and thoughtfully around a score of the Southwest's most inspiring landscapes, from the low desert of California's Joshua Tree National Park to the 9,157-foot peak of Mount Lemmon in Arizona's Santa Catalina Mountains. Geographically, the work for *Vast and Intimate* separates into three sections: deserts; "sky islands," or forested mountains rising from the desert; and the high Colorado Plateau. His idea is to present each place in its vastness, then break that into intimate details that illustrate its richness and complexity. Underlying his effort is the notion that beauty breaks in everywhere, and always it has something to show us.

In a wonderful essay simply titled "Beauty," Scott Russell Sanders argues that we should pay deeper attention to our surroundings "because it gives us a glimpse of the underlying order of things." We need underlying order; we need to know that the ripples in the creek at our feet and the lazy corrugations of the cirrus clouds overhead actually come from a similar place in creation. When we absorb this order, the universe becomes a more comfortable, and a more meaningful, place to live. ■

Vast

INSPIRING IMAGINATION AND DEVOTION

Vast (adj): an immense or boundless expanse or space.

The rippling beauty of White Sands National Monument could look very much like infinity to a lost child.

The first time I saw vastness defined, I was 4 years old. Not surprisingly, it occurred close to home, here in my native Southwest.

My parents had brought me to White Sands National Monument for the day. Although I was growing up nearby in the Chihuahuan Desert of west Texas, this was my first introduction to an authentic dune field, as thrilling to a 4-year-old as a shot at surfing. Which is what I proceeded to do, on the windblown swells of fine, white gypsum in southern New Mexico. While my parents were occupied, I scrambled to the crest of a dune and slid ecstatically down its far side, then attacked a couple or four more. Suddenly an albino universe had swallowed me, and I was lost.

Fifty years later, I remember the moment with searing clarity. The dunes marched forever across the landscape, an army of oscillations in dress whites that obliterated all the landmarks, all the trees, all the people on earth. I was looking at infinity, at least as far as any 4-year-old mind could comprehend it, and it was magnificent and terrifying. It would be nice to claim that I had a rush of primal insight into the nature of God, or at least a stirring of appreciation for the desert's natural architecture, but all I felt was what any ordinary kid would in such a circumstance: panic.

They found me in less than half an hour. The monument wasn't deserted, and I didn't have the legs to wander far. I didn't understand this point until much later, but I had been given my first lesson in the power of landscape to seize the imagination and trigger a transcendent moment.

We measly humans can no more see into infinity than a spadefoot toad can ponder the curvature of the earth, but the sensation of confronting something immeasurably vast and timeless is powerful enough. It remains with us in something deeper than visual memory.

The same feeling came to me while flying over the Grand Canyon in the final moments of twilight, when the shadows inhaled the last trickle of light and the canyon floor melted into a purple void. Our suddenly infinitesimal Cessna seemed profoundly alone — the floor had dropped out of the universe. Humanity's engineering achievements represented in our single-engine aircraft seemed remarkably meager. The sensation occurred again the first time I ventured onto the open Pacific Ocean in my kayak, outside Washington and British Columbia's labyrinths of sheltered straits and island passages. Riding the swells in a 50-pound fiberglass banana, staring into a blue cosmos for which evolution had left me very poorly outfitted for survival, I became infinitely humble. Any other posture would have been ludicrous.

Such emotion occurred repeatedly to John C. Van Dyke, the unlikely Rutgers University librarian and art historian who stumbled around the Southwest at the turn of the 20th century and then wrote *The Desert*, the vivid art appreciation course in what Americans previously had figured to be their continent's wasteland. Halfway through, Van Dyke spends two full chapters

struggling to describe the beauty and emotional impact of the desert's air and sky, then finally collapses in the arms of his own questions:

What is it that draws us to the boundless and the fathomless? Why should the lovely things of earth — the grasses, the trees, the lakes, the little hills — appear trivial and insignificant when we come face to face with the sea or the desert or the vastness of the midnight sky? Is it that the one is the tale of things known and the other merely a hint, a suggestion of the unknown? Or have immensity, space, magnitude a peculiar beauty of their own?

"Peculiar beauty" is certainly a part of the allure of the "boundless and fathomless," but the deeper attraction, I think, has to do with the imagination. Some people prefer to call this the spiritual dimension. But here in the Southwest, sky and mountains are sacred places even to those of us without religion, because they inspire our imagination and devotion — and maybe even our actions.

The literature and culture of the Southwest swarm with examples. The *Navajo Night Chant* unfolds "in the house made of the dawn" and "in the house made of the evening twilight." Hard to imagine a more powerful or evocative stage set for human endeavor. Late in the 19th century, artists such as Thomas Moran helped trigger America's westward migration by painting skies and mountains of epic grandeur, paeans to fresh starts and heroic deeds. In the early 1940s, physicist

J. Robert Oppenheimer came to northern New Mexico prospecting for a site to base the Manhattan Project. He checked out a suggested canyon in the Jemez Mountains but rejected it in favor of the Pajarito Plateau north of Santa Fe, 7,400 feet high in the sky. He felt the scientists developing the atom bomb needed to be able to stare into infinity.

I have known people whose creative spirits needed the great open expanse of the Southwestern sky as much as their lungs needed its oxygen. Judith Chafee, one of Arizona's best architects of the 20th century, grew up in Tucson but migrated to New England for her education and apprenticeship. In 1970 she returned to Tucson and renovated an adobe house downtown as her home and studio. She had been drowning in the "green muck," as she called it, of the Connecticut forests. "I think I will lose myself, my purpose," she explained, "if I can't see something beautifully naked and clear, if I don't see the edge of space on the horizon."

What is this "edge of space?" The Southwestern sky never quite fills the space above earth, stretching into infinity. It may not seem as vast as the Great Plains sky. Here it's an overturned bowl with a randomly broken rim, punctured with mountains, mesas, and the other assorted serrations that form our natural skyline. But these rocky punctuations themselves represent something we desperately crave: stability. Of course mountains move — they thrust up, blow up, tilt, erode, exfoliate, and

ABOVE / Tsé Bit'a'i, the Navajo name for Shiprock, had been scratching the New Mexico sky for some 30 million years before humans ever saw it.
FOLLOWING PAGES / Footprints of a bird become intimate works of art in the dunes of White Sands.

fall down — but this seldom happens on our clock.

"There is nothing like geology to take the urgency out of the morning's news," wrote Scott Russell Sanders. That's the reason, I think, that we embrace mountains. They represent another dimension of vastness: time without end, for all we know.

I moved to Tucson in the early 1970s, as developers were increasingly clawing up the southern flanks of the Santa Catalina Mountains, scraping out roads and pads for expensive homes. If I could have afforded an expensive home I might have bought a piece of the rock myself — I felt an affinity for it, like everyone else — but on a newspaper reporter's salary all I could do was, well, report on the phenomenon. Which I did, rather peevishly. I asked why people are drawn selfishly to mountains, so that they barnacle the slopes with development, obstructing the natural beauty for everyone else.

A psychologist (who lived on the lower slopes of the Catalinas himself) offered an intriguing insight. It wasn't necessarily ego or even the craving for a good view, he speculated. Instead, he said, "Snuggling up to something permanent seems to offer us a connection to permanence ourselves."

Many Southwest writers have concurred. In his New Mexico memoir, *If Mountains Die*, Taos author John Nichols wrote, "As does the ocean, these mountains give the people who live in or near them an especially majestic perspective that helps to enlighten their daily struggles, and offers

them the chance, if they will take it, to be larger than life." More wryly, Charles Bowden wrote in *Frog Mountain Blues*, an angry meditation on those barnacled Catalinas, "We do not know who we are until we look at the mountain."

Shiprock, New Mexico, is a diatreme, geologists' jargon for the esophagus of a violent, volcanic blowout that hardened into a craggy tower. To the Anglo-American imagination, the formation resembles nothing so much as an immense castle, bristling with heaven-storming gables and ramparts scarred and raked from centuries of assaults. This image, however, is a drab cartoon compared to the rock's story as unfolded by the people who know it best, the Navajos.

To the Navajos living around it, *Tsé Bit'a'i*, the rock with wings, once was the home of a pair of nightmarish raptors that resembled gigantic eagles. From this aerie they would swoop down to catch and eat the helpless Navajo people, and they seemed so invincible that the people feared they would soon consume all humanity. But one day Monster Slayer, the child of Changing Woman (the creator of human life), tricked the predators by hiding on the rock until the birds wobbled back to their base in a thunderstorm. Hurling arrows made of lightning, Monster Slayer killed the creatures and saved his people.

Even though crippled by my prosaic Anglo heritage, I can see this titanic struggle taking place on Shiprock's summit. I have driven all around the mountain — no minor excursion, given the reservation's sparse road network — viewing it from all

possible angles, every possible time of day and night. I have peered down on it from Mesa Verde, Colorado, 50 miles away. I have watched the sky frame it in blue, white, orange, red, violet, and black. I have read its geology and its legend, and — I have no rational way to explain this — the two have merged into one, making perfect sense, the natural and the supernatural intertwined.

Maybe we learn who we are by looking at Shiprock. We absorb its beauty and its mystery, use it to anchor a faith in nature's permanence, employ it to invent our culture. Some of us would like to learn who we are by climbing it, but the Navajos declare it strictly off limits. Wisely, because that preserves its sacredness for their culture and its iconic mystery for ours. We need some mountains that can't be climbed.

Infinity and eternity are by definition incomprehensible for us thoroughly finite and terminal creatures. What we instinctively sense as going on forever — desert sky, mountain, dune field — can be chopped down to exact size by modern science. (White Sands is the wind-blown detritus of Pleistocene rock formations in the Sacramento and San Andres mountains; Shiprock is 30 million years old and currently 1,968 feet high.) What we absorb from these earthscapes — what we need — is story. The life-giving energy of a mystery, a romance, a legend. Things that are vast enough to challenge our comprehension are good for us. We get lost in them, and we are richer because of it. ▪

Intimate

CULTIVATING DEEPER EXPERIENCES WITH NATURE

Intimate (adj): marked by very close association, contact, or familiarity.

The geometric patterns of a desert tortoise's carapace and scales form a kind of living geology.

"Hell of a place to lose a cow."

There are several variants on what Ebenezer Bryce, the pioneer Utah homesteader, is supposed to have said about the convoluted fairyland of hoodoos that now wears his name, but they all have to do with cows lurching like pinballs through an endless forest of posts. I can see these hapless bovines in my mind as my wife, Patty, and I slog down a steep trail into the maze. It is a questionable day to be seeking any close association with this landscape. The sky is sulking like wet lead, and the forecast has promised 8 to 12 inches of snow. If the trail gets buried, Bryce Canyon will be a hell of a place to lose a couple of hikers.

But we have a map, a compass, a can of chicken spread, and one of those 2-ounce Mylar "blankets" that allegedly help hikers conserve body heat in the event of an unplanned overnighter. And so we go.

Why? David Roberts wrote that "Anyone who sees a mountain knows at once what the point of it is: to get to the top. It is not so obvious what to do with a canyon."

Maybe this is why so many of us simply drive to Bryce, Canyon de Chelly, or the Grand Canyon and peer in from the safety-railed overlooks. What do we do with a yawning gash in the earth? Design a bridge? Study geology? Simply stand and stare in respectful awe at the colors and geometry of the spectacle?

The latter seems like an appropriate response, but it isn't enough. It doesn't lead to intimacy.

I learned that point some decades ago when I visited the Grand Canyon for the first time as a more-or-less casual tourist. I stared respectfully from several of the programmed overlooks, enjoyed a picnic on a rock cantilevered over the void, and ventured a tentative mile or two down Bright Angel Trail to get the feel of actually being in the canyon.

A few weeks later, writing an unplanned essay about the visit, I struggled. I began to feel like a fraud. When I tried to describe the texture of the Kaibab limestone and Toroweap sandstone of the canyon walls, I drew a blank. I hadn't thought to touch them with my hands. Nor had I looked closely and intently at anything else. No one can claim an intimate knowledge of the entire Grand Canyon, but I didn't seriously know even one cubic foot of it.

So this is why Patty and I are willing to take the modest risk of venturing into the iron oxide labyrinth of Bryce on a bad day. We will be alone in there, it may rough us up a bit, and we will need to be vividly aware of our surroundings. If we are, we will learn something.

Intimate acquaintance with the natural world doesn't necessarily mean lying down flat on the ground and examining things from the vantage of a kangaroo rat, although this exercise can often be useful. In the broader sense, being intimate with the land means cultivating richer, deeper and more focused experiences with nature.

Like most weekend adventurers, I slouch into the natural world as an escape *from* at least as much as an escape *to*. As I hike, I tend to scroll through a private agenda of preoccupations, everything from an assigned article that isn't going well to the world's dwindling petroleum reserves. As long as this nonsense clatters around in my head, nothing short of a bear beside the trail will get my attention. (Amendment: this isn't quite correct. Patty reminds me that two years ago I did fail to notice a bear staring at us, quite intently, from 50 feet away.)

"I am alarmed when it happens that I have walked a mile into the woods bodily, without getting there in spirit," admitted Thoreau. "What business have I in the woods, if I am thinking of something out of the woods?" As usual, Henry was being cranky — as if it were moral trespassing for someone to take a quiet walk in the woods just to saw on a problem — but also, as usual, perceptive. The distracted plod becomes a habit, a norm, and we never learn to see anything that enhances our understanding of the world (which itself might just solve a problem or two).

In fact, all we need to know for effective and even gracious survival on earth we can learn from Nature. This is not a quaint or romantic idea, although in the contemporary hurricane of technology and popular culture it may not seem obvious. Which, I think, is all the more reason to go out there and look — and listen, feel and smell — thoughtfully and intimately.

Nature's lessons operate on two different levels: the practical and the philosophical.

Frank Lloyd Wright first came to Arizona in 1928. His ego already was swollen to its full maturity, a mass roughly the size of Jupiter, but by the time he began building his regional masterpiece, Taliesin West, in 1938, he had deduced an architecture for the desert by *observing* the desert. This was no place for buildings with great, boxlike walls, Wright insisted. He saw that everything from the local rocks and reptiles to the saguaro and cholla cactus had a textured skin or filigree that broke up and scattered the harsh sunlight falling on it. This was both a practical and an aesthetic principle when applied to architecture: buildings could help shade and ornament themselves with changing patterns of sunlight and shadow, and they could slip graciously into the landscape (as Taliesin West does, effortlessly).

"Be quiet — will you — at any cost," he wrote in 1940. "Blot out your clumsy intrusions as you best can. It is the only apology you can make to Arizona."

I often think about architecture when walking in the desert — and more broadly, I think about Nature's implications for the lay and manner of civilization in the desert. We've largely ignored them. This is the philosophical side of the inspiration. The native flora and fauna could teach us to live here within our means. To conserve and recycle. To treasure shade and water. To avoid overwhelming a land that is inherently unsuited for great masses of people. To fold up and take a nap on a hot summer afternoon. To take the inspiration of the intimate and yet extravagant gesture,

ABOVE AND OPPOSITE PAGE / Bryce Canyon National Park in Utah lures explorers into a winter
wonderland.
FOLLOWING PAGES / Creeks and waterfalls are often miniatures in the Southwest, inviting intimate
contemplation. This is Thunder River Spring in the Grand Canyon.

like the soaptree yucca suddenly erupting in the water-gathering swales of a dune field. *Carpe diem*.

We have built civilization in the desert as if we were defying gravity, but gravity cannot be defied — only outwitted, temporarily. Unless we learn to live with the desert environment instead of resisting it, that is what we will be: temporary.

There are other dividends in learning to observe the natural world intimately.

You see patterns at work — patterns that appear again and again in nature, in wildly different contexts, and this helps to make sense of the physical world. The branches of a river system resemble the branches of a tree, which resembles the circulatory system in a leaf. Drying mud flats tend to separate into polyhedrons that look like the patterning of a desert tortoise's shell. The fountainlike throw of a desert lavender bloom is repeated a hundred times larger in the branches of an ocotillo. These are not accidents. Laws of physics and survival dictate natural forms, so they appear wherever they must.

And what all this adds up to is nothing less than the nature of beauty itself. I best absorb beauty when I connect with it on an intellectual level; when I actually understand what it means. I peer into the orange abyss of a barrel cactus's flower, and I am more delighted by its armament of ferociously sharp, curling spines protecting it than I am the richly colored delicacy, because it helps explain the world to me. (It is not because I am a guy, atavistically

itching to play with spears and swords.) Beauty is at its best when it has a reason for being — and in nature, it always does. Always.

And what then? Essayist Scott Russell Sanders replies, "So we answer the beauty we find with the beauty we make." This is what Wright did with Taliesin West; this is what all of us of more modest talents try to do. But absorbing that inspiration has to come first. Without the lessons of nature — without understanding ourselves and our civilization as a part of it — we build on a foundation of nothing more substantial than ego.

The snow begins to fall in Bryce Canyon, exactly as predicted. Fog crowds in with it. The hoodoos around us begin to look like ghostly body parts of mythological creatures, adrift in a gasified primordial milk. Snow clumps on the trees and ledges of the cliffs, forming a brilliant crown to the vermilion and orange of the rock. It also begins to stick, ominously, to the trail.

We look intimately at landmarks, trying to burn them into memory. It doesn't work, because the forms in Bryce Canyon are so far outside our normal frames of reference. I strain to see Snoopy or the Space Shuttle in a hoodoo, but nothing

registers. Still, there is a dividend. I observe fascinating textures in the sandstone, the tree bark, the snow. I begin to understand the process that sculpted this rancher's nightmare (16 million years of river cutting, rain freezing and rock cracking). I begin to know the place.

After a couple of hours, the storm gods have done enough for the day. The overcast parts, a blue hole emerges in the northern sky, and a few moments later the sun begins to bathe the hoodoo garden in quietly elegant light. Birds break out and sing their territorial arias. Snow lodged in the ponderosa pines begins to creak, and then it plops.

We reconnect with our trail by late afternoon. We slog the 900 vertical feet out of the canyon. "Slog" is not an adequate word, though. We are cows learning to surf in mud. Caked in the orange glop, we hit the rim just as the day's last tour bus disgorges its flock. They stare at us as if Mr. and Ms. Sasquatch are oozing out of the canyon before their eyes. They think we are nuts. We think we are the two people on the planet who are fully alive. ■

Harmony

AN IDEAL WORTH PURSUING

Every moment instructs, and every object: for wisdom is infused into every form.
— *Ralph Waldo Emerson*
"Nature"

Yellow columbines seize a foothold in metamorphic rock streaked with quartz in Tucson's upper Sabino Canyon.

Five canyons in four days. An ambitious agenda, but I'm in decent hiking condition and motivated by a passion for these walled-off worlds that go about their secretive business within half an hour's drive from the middle of Tucson. No other city in North America is so richly defined by its natural surroundings, and these rambling, V-shaped clefts in the Santa Catalina Mountains enclose an amazing variety of spectacles.

I once walked (more than a little nervously) alongside a herd of javelinas in one of these canyons, and sat on a ledge in another and listened to a polyphonic concert of ephemeral waterfalls crashing through the desert. I have seen bobcats, Gila monsters, a probably bewildered great blue heron, and numerous varieties of rattlesnakes. I have noted the effects of flash floods and severe drought, both of which are just business as usual in the long term of a desert mountain canyon.

I revisit my favorite canyons in the mountain's south-facing front range: Bear, Ventana, Finger Rock, Pima — a corrugation of fissures and ridges "laid out side by side like a bony hand," as botanist Janice Emily Bowers perfectly describes their configuration. The canyons seem little changed from when I moved away from Tucson five years earlier, but "little changed," in this case, does not have the ring of perfect reassurance.

The Santa Catalinas may look virtually the same geologically since the first humans wandered into their shadows some 11,500 years ago, but their biology has changed substantially. In just the last century the grizzly and the gray wolf disappeared from these mountains, casualties of the human tide lapping at their base. The last survey of bighorn sheep in 1994 found a population of only a dozen, not nearly enough to be a viable reproducing herd. One theory maintains that brush buildup from fire suppression has been helping mountain lions pounce on the sheep more effectively; others blame habitat intrusion by houses and hikers. One way or another, the herd's demise connects to our increased presence.

On my last day in Tucson I drive to the Catalinas' backside, as Tucsonans used to refer to the north slopes. The Romero Canyon trail back here used to be one of my favorites — remote enough to be almost private, providing alternating vast and intimate vistas as it snakes between ridge and canyon into the Pusch Ridge Wilderness. Three miles in — my destination — lies Romero Pools, a maze of sensuously grotesque rocks that look like a fountain sculpted by Henry Moore. We native desert rats have some primal homing device that will cause us to cheerfully undertake any grinding hike in order to sit on a rock beside a washtub-sized pool of water supplied by a seasonal trickle. The simple fact that such an oasis exists, that it perseveres in the face of the desert's long odds, seems reassuring.

Before the trail curls down toward the pools, it climbs a spiny ridge providing a grand view of the Cañada del Oro basin more than a thousand feet below and — to my surprise, a whole new piece of city. In the few years I'd been away, Tucson had flooded around the mountain, oozing into the shape of a vast horseshoe, collaring the mountains that used to form its northern wall. From the ridge I can hear the tireless throb of civilization several miles away, a mumbled commotion of engines, tires and assorted machinery, most of the latter, my binoculars reveal, busily engaged in digging and grading to make still more city.

Urban growth in the American Southwest over the last half-century has been phenomenal. In 1970 Tucson's metro population was roughly 322,000; in 2000 it was 834,000. Metropolitan Las Vegas recently has been nearly doubling in size every 10 years. In 1995 *The Arizona Republic* noted that suburban Phoenix was spreading into the desert at the rate of an acre every hour. Friends of development may punch up the math and point out that at this rate it would take 8,219 years for the metropolis to fill up Arizona, but the exercise misses the point. We are colonizing so much of our once-wild land that we are in danger of losing our connections to nature, and altering the balance of what wilderness remains.

This is not a rabid environmentalist's rant. Each of the three houses I successively occupied in Tucson gobbled its own quarter-acre of desert, rendering that land essentially uninhabitable for most native species. I gladly use the paved roads that pierce the Santa Catalinas, the Chiricahuas, Oak Creek Canyon, and dozens of other hard and rocky places. To deny access and improvement not only amounts to hypocrisy but also denies civilization and the nature of humanity itself. This is who we are, this is what we do, for better or for worse.

In a rich and perceptive book titled *The Edges of the Civilized World*, poet and essayist Alison Hawthorne Deming writes about her travels in increasingly less remote Baja California, about feeling "how fragile wildness has become. I had been traveling not in the wilderness, it seemed, but along the edges of the civilized world — a fault line where pressure constantly builds, where the impingement of economic necessity abrades against nature."

Actually, the abrasion rubs both ways. The human connection to the natural environment has long been a colossal shoving match, an eternal thrust on our end to render that environment controllable and comfortable, and a mightily stubborn push back from nature to reclaim the upper hand. Nature grows the crops she chooses without apparent effort, but a human gardener has to keep endless vigil with a hoe and chemical arsenal. A construction crew can blade a mountain slope and build a luxury home in a few months, but a brushfire or a flash flood can undo it all in a few minutes. A city of 834,000 can spring up in the desert, but when its water finally runs out, the creosote, cactus wren, and coyote will patiently repopulate whatever ruins we leave. They will remember how to live here.

If we hope to be more than very temporary residents, we will need to look more closely at this natural world we keep shoving ourselves into, understand it more

ABOVE / Even in death, the wavelike curves and rippling textures of bristlecone pines form a beautiful composition.
OPPOSITE PAGE / A frog resting on rock in Sabino Canyon gives us harmony blending line, color, and light.
FOLLOWING PAGES / Artistic patterns like this arrangement of rocks and water emerge in Arizona's Oak Creek.

thoroughly, and appreciate it more deeply — and maybe reconsider some of our grand schemes for it.

We have a wisdom to absorb from nature, as Emerson wrote. Infused in everything we look at — the infinite views and intimate details alike — that wisdom, it seems to me, can be expressed in one word: harmony.

In music, harmony is created when two or more notes sound together as a chord or intersect as contrapuntal lines. Through most of the last thousand years of Western music, chords have been pleasing to our ears. If they were dissonant, the accepted rules of composition insisted they be resolved quickly into consonance. (The 20th century threw these rules out on their ear, but now they're back, and that's all to the good.) In art and architecture, harmony involves color, balance, and proportion. If we're not technically schooled in these arts, we may not know why something feels wrong, but we know instinctively when it does, and it makes us feel uneasy.

Harmony exists everywhere in Nature, even if it isn't immediately apparent, and the systems are sometimes exceedingly complex. A mountain lion kills a bighorn sheep and gnaws on the remains for a day or two, then walks away in disgust — cats dislike decaying meat. But bears, coyotes, vultures, and ants don't seem to mind it, and within a few days the bones are picked clean, abandoned to become a Georgia O'Keeffe sculpture bleaching in the sun, not only fulfilling a purpose but also registering a certain nobility in death. Nothing is wasted, nothing is regretted.

Native American religion frequently centers on the ideal of harmony — in Navajo the word *hozho* encompasses the concept of harmony with Nature, with human relationships, with tradition. Still, this is an ideal, not necessarily reality. Evidence is mounting that even prehistoric people dramatically shifted Nature's balance on the new continents they invaded: The fossil record reveals that most of the big herbivores such as mammoths, mastodons, camels, and ground sloths became extinct in the Americas within 1,200 years after the appearance of humans, the only animal that ever learned to throw a spear.

These ancient people probably failed to realize the consequences of their actions, so it's hard to blame them. In our time, with modern science and communications, the failure is more difficult to explain. Untrammeled beauty is its own reward, the preservation of species is a provably urgent priority, and hardly anybody itches to argue with the philosophical concept of deeper harmony with the natural world. So why are we beating it up?

In the late 1940s, a forester and game manager named Aldo Leopold worked on a small collection of essays on such oddly diverse topics as the migration of the upland plover from Argentina to Wisconsin, Nature's uses for diseased trees, and the elegance of hunting with a longbow. Leopold died in 1948, fighting a brush fire on a neighbor's farm, but his son finished editing the manuscripts and had them published the next year under the title *A Sand County Almanac*. It became a classic, introducing a generation to the unfamiliar word *ecology*. Leopold, easily as peevish as Thoreau, believed that we were becoming estranged from Nature because of "innumerable physical gadgets." (He detested jeeps, outboard motors, and especially camping trailers.) He felt we were growing selfish and careless and out of harmony with Nature because we no longer knew her. The essence of his argument was contained in these two graciously crafted sentences:

A thing is right when it tends to preserve the integrity, stability, and beauty of the biotic community. It is wrong when it tends otherwise.

And in these two more:

We abuse land because we regard it as a commodity belonging to us. When we see land as a community to which we belong, we may begin to see it with love and respect. ∎

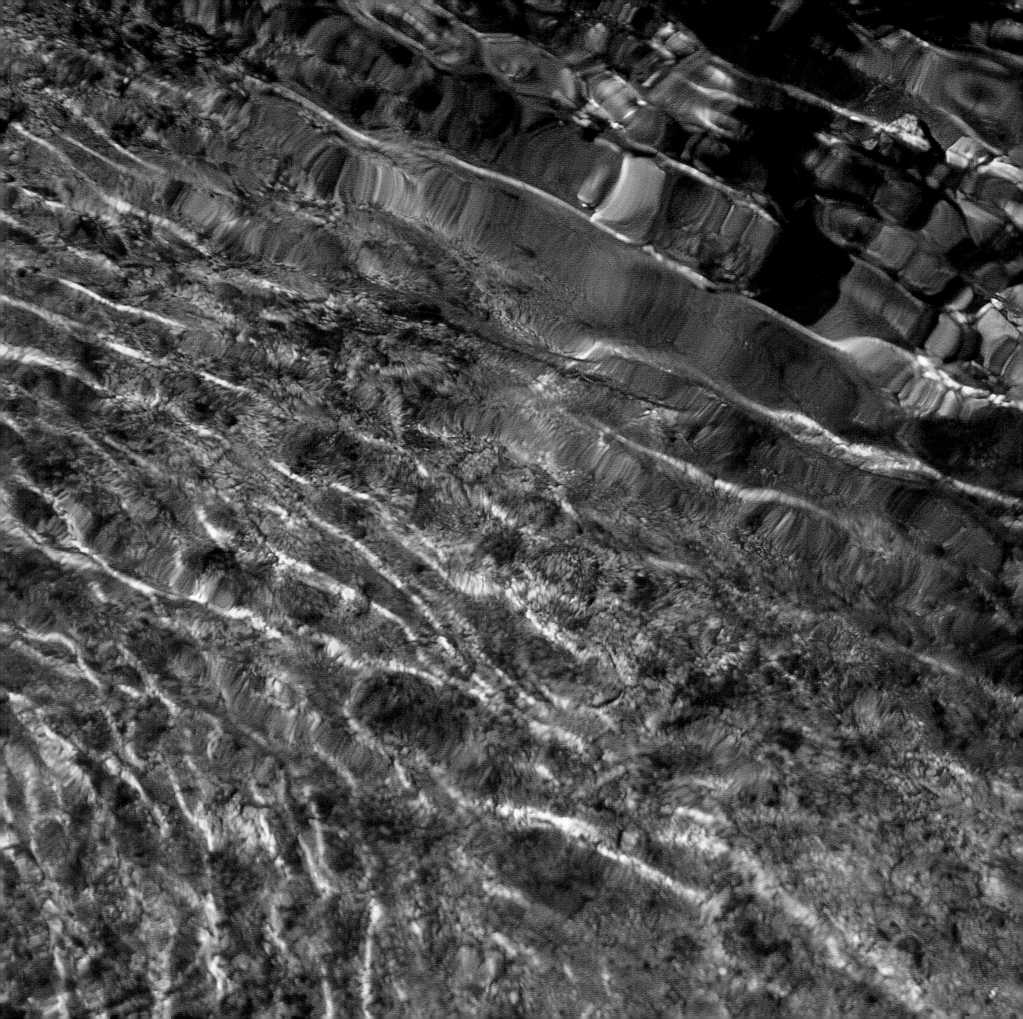

The Sky Islands

Vast & Intimate **PORTFOLIO**

When geologic tumult thrusts a mountain range thousands of feet above a desert basin, a kind of island is born — a self-contained biosphere where life exists with little reference to the arid, essentially flat land surrounding it. A few creatures, such as the irrepressible coyote, may commute freely upslope and down, but many others live out their well-adapted lives with no desire (nor ability) to push the envelope of their world. They may even evolve into subspecies distinct from their relatives on another "island" just a few dozen miles away.

Southern Arizona's sky islands rise as high as Mount Graham's 10,717 feet; New Mexico's Mogollon Range tops out at 10,892 feet. The mountains harbor national forests and national monuments, prehistoric ruins, astronomical observatories, peaks sacred to modern native peoples, and everywhere, a cornucopia of natural magnificence.

Nature can move abruptly on sky islands — sometimes stretching zones over only a hundred feet before changing flora and fauna patterns. Or it can move slowly, requiring hundreds of thousands of years before change manifests itself.

Sky islands can nurture vibrant life (Mount Graham, top, and Mount Lemmon) and also hold sacred meaning (Baboquivari, opposite page).

Baboquivari Peak The profile of its craggy crown, viewed from the Altar Valley of southern Arizona and northern Sonora, is unforgettable: a bulbous dome with a protruding button, a classic teapot or gigantic tangelo.

But these are a white man's metaphors, and Baboquivari Peak has a far richer meaning to the Tohono O'odham, People of the Desert, living in its shadow. It is their sacred mountain, spiritual center of their universe and home to I'itoi, the Elder Brother and protector of the people.

BABOQUIVARI PEAK

BABOQUIVARI PEAK

BABOQUIVARI PEAK

Chiricahua Mountains This range commands superlatives: the most massive of the southern Arizona sky islands, the most geologically exotic, the most biologically diverse. Four major ecosystems converge on it: the Sierra Madre to the south, the Chihuahuan and Sonoran deserts on the east and west, and the Rocky Mountains to the north. Within the Chiricahuas, or outside tugging at its skirts, are plants and animals from all those dramatically diverse communities.

From exposed peaks, the Chiricahuas offer vast views of desert basins and mountains 50 miles away; but they also harbor hidden landscapes of Lilliputian streams and bark furrowed with miniature organic canyons. The Apache words for the range, which the Spaniards spelled as best they could, rightly describes it: *tsil*, meaning "mountain," and *kawa*, "great."

RUSTLER PARK, CHIRICAHUA MOUNTAINS

CAVE CREEK, CHIRICAHUA MOUNTAINS

CHIRICAHUA MOUNTAINS

VIEW FROM THE PINALENOS

Pinaleno Mountains

Mount Graham, the highest place in southern Arizona at 10,717 feet, is famous for astronomy and controversy. The University of Arizona operates two observatories on the Pinalenos' peak, a favorable site for its dry air and minimal light pollution. But Apaches and environmentalists have bitterly opposed the machinery. The mountain is sacred to the Indians, and it is vital habitat to the endangered Mount Graham red squirrel, a subspecies unique to the Pinaleno conifer forests above 7,800 feet. For those not looking for a fight, the biological and landform beauties of this sky island are engaging enough.

PINALENO MOUNTAINS

SANTA CATALINA MOUNTAINS

Santa Catalina Mountains

f the city of Tucson can be said to have a soul, it is here, in this gneiss-and-granite mountain range towering over a city that seems increasingly determined to encircle it. The range draws a jagged skyline defining the city's northern horizon and establishing direction — in the obvious geographical sense, and maybe by the spiritual compass as well.

The lone road up Mount Lemmon, the Santa Catalinas' highest peak, leads summer-weary Tucsonans to cool, forested relief within 30 minutes of leaving the city. But the Santa Catalinas offer far more to those who come to know them intimately: a quiet retreat, constant lessons in humility, and lifelong studies of Nature's exquisitely managed gearworks.

SANTA CATALINA MOUNTAINS

SANTA CATALINA MOUNTAINS

SANTA CATALINA MOUNTAINS

SANTA CATALINA MOUNTAINS

SANTA CATALINA MOUNTAINS

Santa Rita Mountains

Public roads only poke at the mountains' edges, and the Smithsonian observatory nestled in the range generates little commotion. Hikers cherish the Santa Ritas for the profusion of wildlife and the bald summit — unique among southern Arizona's sky islands — of 9,453-foot Mount Wrightson.

Edward Abbey defined wilderness as a place where there are creatures that can eat you. Janice Emily Bowers characterized it as a place without a script, where one is "at the mercy of wild chance." In season in the Santa Ritas, one will accidentally encounter lovely, pint-sized brooks, marked on no map. Bears are not uncommon, either.

SANTA RITA MOUNTAINS

SANTA RITA MOUNTAINS

SANTA RITA MOUNTAINS

The Colorado Plateau

Vast & Intimate **PORTFOLIO**

This vast, sparsely populated landscape is no place to stumble around in the dark. Geology rules in this 130,000-square-mile basin ringed by mountains. One faulty step could mean a plunge into a canyon hundreds of feet deep, or thousands. In the other direction are pinnacles, volcanoes, and sandstone monoliths too steep (or too sacred) to be climbed reasonably. The forms are a testament to Nature's endless talent for drama — and occasionally comedy.

Navajos will tell you there are prehistoric ruins, major ones that not even archaeologists have found, deep in their backcountry (though they certainly won't tell you where). The Grand Canyon will inform you that you are infinitesimal, a speck in both space and time. But the palpable hazards, the nagging mysteries, the absolute certainty of having a humbling experience, only enhance the allure of this plateau ranging over parts of Arizona, Utah, New Mexico, and Colorado. Certain places remind us that our imagination is too small; this is one of them.

Canyonlands National Park (top and opposite page) bears vegetation of an arid land and geologic formations of a weathered plateau. But Oak Creek Canyon at the plateau's base has lusher plant life (bottom).

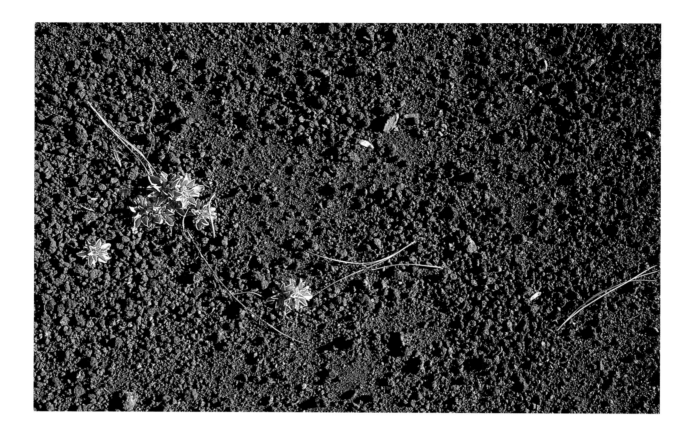

Sunset Crater / San Francisco Peaks

Northern Arizona's volcano field is a riot of color — wild buckwheat and golden rabbit brush erupting from black cinders at Sunset Crater Volcano National Monument, aspens drinking the late autumn sunlight on the slopes of the nearby San Francisco Peaks, and soft sandstone formations slowly eroding into the characteristic salmon sand of the Colorado Plateau. The last volcanic event here occurred nearly a millennium ago, barely a moment in geologic time, but life — as always — has flourished in its aftermath.

SAN FRANCISCO PEAKS

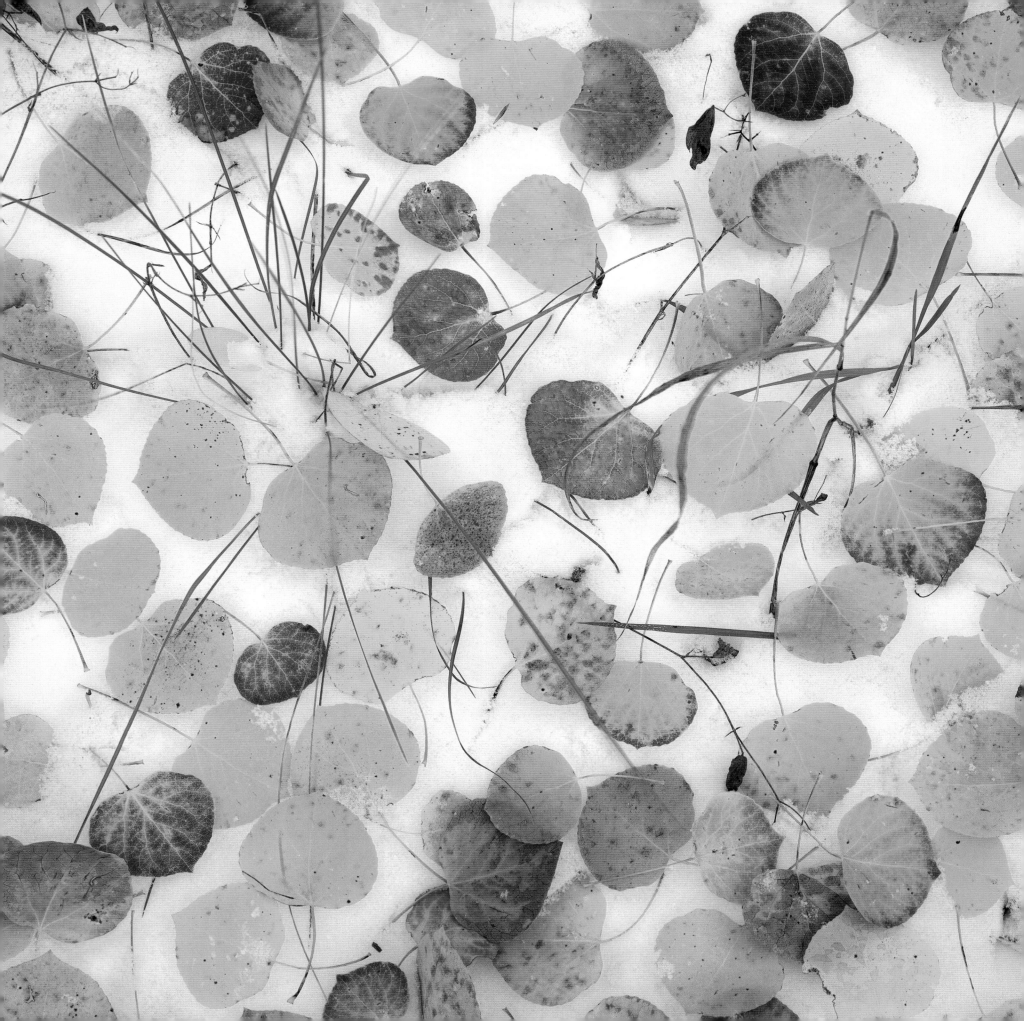

SAN FRANCISCO PEAKS

SAN FRANCISCO PEAKS

SAN FRANCISCO PEAKS

Arches / Canyonlands national parks Sandstone performs magic in southern Utah. It cracks, flakes, crumbles, and weathers into impossible arches (more than 1,500 in the catalog of Arches National Park alone), and erodes into canyons, scalloped escarpments, and fairyland hoodoos. The scale of the natural sculptures at first seems immense, but Nature's art occurs in the intimate range as well.

ARCHES NATIONAL PARK

GREEN RIVER OVERLOOK, CANYONLANDS NATIONAL PARK

DELICATE ARCH, ARCHES NATIONAL PARK

CANYONLANDS NATIONAL PARK

BALANCED ROCKS, ARCHES NATIONAL PARK

ARCHES / CANYONLANDS NATIONAL PARKS

AQUA CANYON, BRYCE CANYON NATIONAL PARK

Bryce Canyon National Park

The gentle Paria River and its tributaries, flowing across the Paunsaugunt Plateau, wreaked this geologic havoc. The water cut deep gullies into the sedimentary rock, worked itself into cracks, froze and expanded, and then the expansion popped off chips and slabs to form the wacky spires, minarets and cartoon-character forms we call hoodoos. The construction — or, more accurately, destruction — continues; in a few more million years the entire formation will erode into oblivion.

Chaco Canyon

This site — Chaco Culture National Historic Park — in northwestern New Mexico ranks as the most eerie and baffling prehistoric settlement in North America. Between A.D. 850 and 1150 the Anasazi built more than a dozen "great houses" here, pueblos up to five stories high with as many as 800 rooms and dozens of circular kivas. Logs for ceiling beams had to be dragged from forests at least 25 miles away, and millions of sandstone blocks had to be shaped and laid. But for what purpose? The canyon is notoriously inhospitable; its meager resources could not possibly have supported a large population.

Even in ruin, the architecture exudes a sense of power and nobility. The buildings are crafted with great skill and care. That we don't know why only deepens Chaco's allure.

CHACO CANYON

Grand Canyon National Park No one has
ever said it
more aptly, or
more grandly,
than John Wesley Powell, who
led two expeditions through it on
the Colorado River: The Grand
Canyon is "the most sublime
spectacle on the earth."

TOROWEAP POINT, GRAND CANYON

CHUAR BUTTE, GRAND CANYON

DEER CREEK, GRAND CANYON / FOLLOWING PAGES, HERMIT RAPIDS ON COLORADO RIVER

GRAND CANYON

GRAND CANYON

RIBBON FALLS, GRAND CANYON

TOROWEAP POINT, GRAND CANYON

Grand Staircase - Escalante National Monument

Only in 1996 did southern Utah's wild and lonely land marked by dramatic cliffs, twisting canyons, sheer pinnacles, and graceful arches receive permanent protection as a national monument. Hiking into its 1.7-million-acre wilderness reveals ancient history. There are dinosaur fossils and Anasazi rock art. The "staircase" is indeed the world's grandest, a natural ziggurat of gray, white, and vermilion cliffs that rises 5,000 feet to the lip of Bryce Canyon.

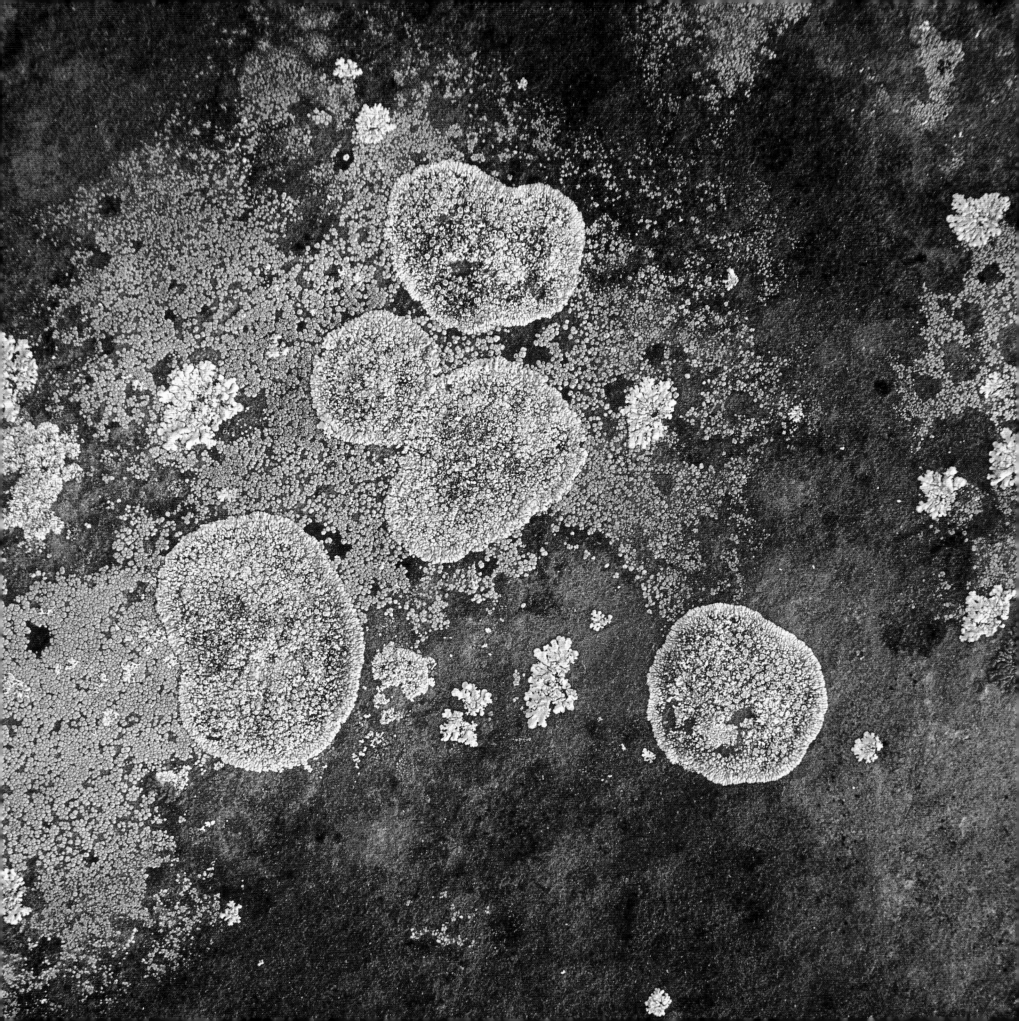

GRAND STAIRCASE - ESCALANTE

SUNSET ARCH, GRAND STAIRCASE - ESCALANTE

MONUMENT VALLEY

Monument Valley Navajo Tribal Park

No other landscape declares itself "the West" as firmly and distinctly as Monument Valley, the great collection of sandstone totems straddling the Arizona-Utah border. It has become almost a cliché, the backdrop for countless Western movies and truck commercials. But on intimate acquaintance the landscape becomes newly rewarding, rich with unexpected forms and colors that change as light and shadows roll over it.

MONUMENT VALLEY

FOLLOWING PAGES, THE MITTENS FORMATIONS, MONUMENT VALLEY

Red Rock Country "Wild, violent, savage," one of Zane Grey's Old West characters described Oak Creek Canyon in *The Call of the Canyon.* Today's visitor to the landscape around Sedona often referred to as Red Rock Country hardly will discern such a temperament in the canyon, one of the Southwest's most civilized natural wonders. Three million visitors a year ply the snaking road that parallels the creek on the canyon floor — their numbers peaking around mid-October when leaves turn to red and gold. Oak Creek's West Fork hike has become one of Arizona's most popular. Happily, it is possible to enjoy wildness in the nearby Red Rock-Secret Mountain and Sycamore Canyon wildernesses and on the less traveled trails up the canyon slopes and tributaries.

RED ROCK COUNTRY

RED ROCK COUNTRY

RED ROCK COUNTRY

RED ROCK COUNTRY

Paria Canyon / Vermilion Cliffs

Our planet's most dramatic geology conveniently gathers along a narrow strip stretching some 75 miles south and 50 miles north of the Arizona-Utah border. The Paria Canyon and River and the Vermilion Cliffs rank among the region's most striking forms. The slot canyons and ruddy ramparts here are not nearly as famous as Zion, Bryce, and the Grand Canyon, but their beauty rewards an intimate exploration. The land is lonely and challenging. Nature entertains here on her own terms — which is as it should be.

ECHO PEAKS, VERMILION CLIFFS

VERMILION CLIFFS

EARTH PATTERNS, PARIA CANYON / CLOUD-DRAPED VERMILION CLIFFS

PARIA CANYON

PARIA CANYON

PARIA CANYON

PARIA CANYON / FOLLOWING PAGES, VERMILION CLIFFS

VERMILION CLIFFS

SHIPROCK

Shiprock This spike-knuckled diatreme, the eroded remnant of a volcanic feeder pipe, thrusts out of the San Juan Basin like a fist smashing through paper, inspiring awe and respect. At an age of 30 million years, it is also a mountain smashing through geologic time, eternal and changeless in human memory. Not surprisingly, it figures prominently in Navajo legend. Visitors may dream of scaling it, but dream is all they may do: In the Navajo view, a 1939 Sierra Club foray profaned the sacred rock.

SHIPROCK

SHIPROCK

TEMPLE OF SINAWAVA, ZION NATIONAL PARK

Zion National Park This is the New Testament of Colorado Plateau geology, a mere 150 million years old. Zion was written in the same time-honored way as the Grand Canyon: by the patient gnawing of the Virgin River and the freeze-thaw chipping away of the plateau's Navajo sandstone. However, the Grand Canyon exposes rocks 2 billion years old.

Zion offers drama in many forms, from the sheer 2,000-foot walls of the main canyon to the miniature hanging gardens nourished by seeps and springs. Perhaps in no other place are the vast and the intimate so closely intertwined.

FOLLOWING PAGES, KOLOB CANYONS, ZION NATIONAL PARK

ZION NATIONAL PARK

ZION NATIONAL PARK

The Deserts

Vast & Intimate **PORTFOLIO**

Deserts are not wastelands. Nor are they bleak, lonely, unproductive, or unforgiving. Only lifeforms that are not adapted to desert conditions find them hostile. *Homo sapiens* is the only resident species ever heard complaining about the heat. Deserts *are* places of extreme conditions that have inspired extreme biological responses — which is the prime reason that we find deserts so strange and wonderful.

They reward contemplation. Somehow they inspire creative thought and action. Judith Chafee, one of Arizona's greatest modern architects, returned to her native Tucson from New England to practice because she felt herself drowning in the "green muck" of the forests. She needed the clarity of long views and naked land.

Edward Abbey wrote that the great quality of the desert was a strangeness that the human sensibility cannot fully assimilate — but that once you begin trying, "you become a prospector for life, condemned, doomed, exalted."

A cactus blooms and a delicate flower flourishes in desert settings.
Elsewhere, opposite page, Mesquite Flat dunes dominate a Death Valley scene.

Death Valley National Park

Nine mountain ranges guard California's Death Valley from invasion by rain-bearing storms — but once in a while the hills fall asleep on the job and North America's lowest, hottest, driest desert briefly sports a shallow lake on its vast salt pan. Under the moon, the lonely beauty of such an anomaly seems miraculous.

Death Valley's sheer starkness is its prime attraction. Its shadows have edges like razors, the glaze of the ground is blinding, the creases of the mountains are unsoftened by the haze of vegetation. Only the color of the sky, a deep, penetrating blue that seems to envelop infinity, reminds us that we're still walking on planet Earth.

TELESCOPE PEAK AT BADWATER, DEATH VALLEY

DEATH VALLEY

MESQUITE FLAT DUNES, DEATH VALLEY

EUREKA VALLEY DUNES, DEATH VALLEY

MESQUITE FLAT DUNES, DEATH VALLEY

Joshua Tree National Park

One Western explorer, John C. Frémont, called it "the most repulsive tree in the vegetable kingdom." Another, William Manly, thought it was "a brave little tree to live in such a barren country." Aesthetic judgments aside, both men were wrong in appraising it as a tree: Yucca brevifolia, despite growing up to 40 feet high, is a member of the lily family.

The Joshua tree grows only in the cooler and wetter microclimates of the Mojave Desert in California and Arizona. Its eponymous national park, created in 1994, lies at a junction of the Sonoran and Mojave deserts — hence the great profusion of brave little cacti, succulents and, yes, actual trees, in its various botanical zones.

MOUNT SANGORGONIO, JOSHUA TREE NATIONAL PARK

JOSHUA TREE NATIONAL PARK

JOSHUA TREE NATIONAL PARK

Mohave National Preserve

John C. Van Dyke, the turn-of-the-century roamer who turned Americans' disdain of their deserts into respect and fascination, made one glaring error in his lovely 1901 book, *The Desert*. "Aside from the blossoms upon bush [like the yucca at right] and tree there are few bright petals shining in the desert," he proclaimed. "It is no place for flowers. They are too delicate and are usually wanting in tap root and armor."

Van Dyke's three years in the Southwest likely coincided with a dry spell suppressing spring wildflowers. Such dearths can last a decade. Van Dyke, unfortunately, missed one critical facet of the desert's character: its delicacy.

PROVIDENCE MOUNTAINS, MOHAVE NATIONAL PRESERVE

KELSO DUNES, MOHAVE NATIONAL PRESERVE

ANZA-BORREGO DESERT STATE PARK

Anza-Borrego Desert State Park Serious desert is entrenched here in California's San Diego County: four species of rattlesnakes, craggy mountains and bony badlands, a skinflint seven inches of rain in an average year, and an all-time high temperature of 121 degrees.

Yet wildflowers abound, and nestled in the crook of a stony canyon is one of the Southwest's most unusual oases, a crowd of nearly 1,000 California fan palms nurtured by a year-around spring. A desert presents a demanding environment, but not a forbidding one.

Kofa National Wildlife Refuge

Spanish speakers have a colorful word for places like this western Arizona chunk of ruggedness — *despoblado*, a place where no one lives. This is just as well for the bighorn sheep, now numbering close to 1,000, and other reclusive Kofa residents such as the desert iguana, mountain lion, and kit fox. Visitors usually never encounter these creatures — the "refuge," created in 1939 by President Roosevelt, is just that — but the brilliant colors of the prickly pear and ocotillo and the backdrop of the impossibly spiky Kofa Mountains are reward enough.

KOFA NATIONAL WILDLIFE REFUGE

KOFA NATIONAL WILDLIFE REFUGE

Picacho Peak State Park

The desert wildflower bloom is one of Nature's lotteries, a complicated crapshoot that depends on the timing of winter rains, the previous year's blooms, the seed-eating rodent population, and other factors that maybe no one fully understands. Even professional botanists admit that predicting a good bloom is almost impossible until it begins.

When Arizona wildflowers have one of those flings, though, the lower slopes of Picacho Peak become a vast skirt of Mexican gold poppies. It's one of the Southwest's most extravagant seasonal displays, a pageant of sheer joy.

PICACHO PEAK STATE PARK

Organ Pipe Cactus National Monument

f the more familiar saguaro cactus strikes a pose like a referee signaling a touchdown, the organ pipe resembles, well, a cluster of organ pipes reaching for the heavens. The spiny stems grow as high as 20 feet, producing pale lavender flowers that open only at night for intimate visits with long-nosed bats.

ORGAN PIPE CACTUS NATIONAL MONUMENT

ORGAN PIPE CACTUS NATIONAL MONUMENT

Cabeza Prieta National Wildlife Refuge

Cabeza Prieta, the "dark head" of the desert: a mountain Ann Zwinger memorably described as "a pyramid of pearly-tan schist draped with a hangman's hood of black lava;" a wildlife refuge created in 1939; an Air Force gunnery range; a fiercely hot, stony, thorny, angular landscape where a network of *tinajas* — natural depressions in stone that conserve scarce rainwater — sustains wildlife through months of drought.

Through this place runs *El Camino del Diablo*, the Devil's Highway, a route taken by early-day explorers. Now, as then, the place is ominous and foreboding, teeming with life and improbable beauty.

CABEZA PRIETA

Sierra del Pinacate The Pinacate wilderness, a national reserve in Mexico, artfully mixes a starkly beautiful desert of ferocious heat, black cinders, and a unique form of volcanic crater called a maar. Geologists believe that magma rose to the surface and collided with groundwater, creating pressurized steam explosions that would rival today's nuclear weapons blasts. The largest of the resulting craters is a mile wide and 750 feet deep.

MACDOUGAL CRATER, SIERRA DEL PINACATE